I admire...
(Who Or What Do You Admire?)

I will never forget the moment I felt alive for the first time in a long while.

Thank you for making me feel a part of this heartache of a world.

Someone I admire.

Chapters Of Admiration

Loved By A Poet's Tongue

Burned Fables

My Lullaby

Roses Carry Daggered Thorns

Majestic Destinations

Wisdom Of The Young

Dear readers,

A moment graces every human where we feel obligated to choose who to be in that exact time. Forgetting we are allowed to simmer in our faith and our beliefs to truly understand the ingredients in our blood. We forget we are someone to admire. Months passed along with the phases of the moon; times seem to be getting easier. Perhaps I am allowing myself to heal from my own transcript. Life is the most complicated journey we will ever endure. Even death makes more sense than why we are put on this Earth. Maybe we will never know. But as long as our veins run like road maps in our body, we must find a reason to keep going. The world can be so unforgiving, changing unpredictably just when you start figuring things out. Yet just like every tide that fades over the coarse sand, somedays the ripples expand to amounts bigger than any human. While other days are small rocks plummeting to the bottom never to be reached again. I found that life becomes easier when that rope we hold onto slowly slips away, and possibly the scars will still remain from holding on too tight. But at least then we can say that we are free. Find the people that embrace your existence. Find the better part of yourself that knows you just want to be the good, we all have it dwelling deep down waiting for the chance to rise. Some moments will be worthwhile experiencing. Trust me, I am proud I have gotten to live this long. I am grateful to have made another collection of poetry that was released by my inner child and helped me identify more of my character. Poems that come alive like they are more than just stories but pieces of paper that grow legs and learn how to heal those around. I hope this journey will unlock something within your soul, something hidden away in the cages of your ribs that must bleed out. It is too uncomfortable to carry unwanted pain when someone so special as you don't deserve that. We shall go through these pages together; you will never be alone. So, let's find something new together deep in the heart of the forest which guards our souls carefully. I hope you enjoy this collection of soft poetry as much as I did writing it. It means a lot that I have made it this far. I wonder where we will go next? Let's find out.

-Novalee Burkett

Loved By A Poet's Tongue

A charming life

I am besotted with the nature
outside my window.
I look to the awakened day to find the
poetics of life,
only if you open your eyes to see the
words the sky bleeds.
It's pretty like my favorite movie,
a cinematic masterpiece.
It's my favorite quote burned into
the silhouettes of tree bark.
Symphonies directing in
strong dynamics when I see the sun,
as the music slowly
dies to a faint whisper
when night falls.
A nostalgic sentiment as we walk down
this lone road past all
the playsets and dying laughter.
The feeling of life returning
to what it once was,
is something our heart aches for
but can't find the words to say,

"I miss it".
Only truly understanding how we have
grown once we pause to
watch the leaves settle
and realize we can reflect upon it.
Perhaps life isn't poetic at all.
But it feels more human to express
emotions through visions of locution.

Victorian feelings

My knees drop to
the soaked slippery stone.
I appear to be the Devil,
because no one else would
sit upon the wistful rain.
My lungs burn of your name,
my arms pulling invisible
strings from the sky.
Newspapers rolling like tumbleweeds
in the abandoned streets.
My poor pockets jingle of a few coins,
though if I'm honest,
no worth will replace your absence.
Eyes glare beyond the foggy windows
as I whisper my apologies.
A titanium ring bears my finger
for the promise we keep.
The castle I stand beside,
knows none of the pain of
the prisoners they hold.
None of us had done wrong.
We were just medieval fools,

who were too afraid to do what's right.
Please tell me there's a savior
with a halo to fix all the sin we breathe.
If it shall not change in this lifetime,
I will write of my Victorian feelings.
Hoping it gets better
in some other generation.

Cabin crushes

White daisies lead the way towards
the soft glow of the domestic forest.
The navy felt sky peering down
as we skip hand in hand
into the unknown.
A jade gown pinned to you well,
as the ends flow with
every eloquent movement.
A white blouse tucks into
my leather dark pants,
as if we are a walking storybook.
The air is bittersweet like salty
cherries roaming the wind.
Damp soil becomes a roving scent
near a candlelit cabin.
Twisted green vines strangle
the rotting oak boards that
create this timely hideout.
I saw your smile spread like wild fire
as you pull me along inside.
I let you explore,
my heart beating too fast

wouldn't let me stop you.
Behind all the cobwebs
and dust particles,
I saw home.
I took your hand that fit well in mine,
and we danced to no tunes,
but the ones playing in our heads.
We were in our own
little fantasy world.
Quaint,
we found the moment charming.
We were meant for this cabin.

Home

The burning temptation of meeting you
in the broken midnight.
The passion of dark colors
splattered across the sky.
The face of a criminal ready
to steal the moon.
A shallow voice ringing in
my ear not to get closer.
But my hands fit perfectly on the
steering wheel.
The universe had pulled
me to a new cradle.
A strange dream that I
thought could never be.
There are new colors in my iris
and new blood rushing to my cheeks.
A petty nightmare washed away in a
sea of monstrous souls.
I thought home was somewhere to stay,
realizing it's in everything we love.
I'm tired of moving.

Moving oil painting

Dark circles drip from her eyes
like an oil painting of a
raccoon melting in the sun.
Footsteps of a ghost along a trail
to find a wallowing man
haunted by his past.
A kid driving fast on a one headlight
motorcycle under the moon to escape
the insufferable thoughts the town had
left as threats.
Merciful pain clouding the thoughts
of lovers who were shunned away by
their blood now hear the ringing of
wedding bells surrounded
by peace of doves.
The old woman feeding ducks by the
pond still grieving over that
day with her son,
she still sees the reflection
of memories in the water.
An artist will never paint a portrait
without a hidden mistake.

Yet we yearn for our eyes to meet
the masterpiece hung in museums.
Because the most beautiful paintings
are the ones that bleed
raw emotion and flaw.

Beautiful humans

A beautiful meadow stands
neighborly towards hell.
While miserable mortals
are caught in the middle.
Believing that they are not
deserving of something sweet.
And perhaps we aren't.
Sitting by the haunted campfire
that attracts our tired eyes like moths.
We sing tales of tragedy
and melodies of regret.
Hoping the souls around that are
engulfed by the heat will
mend our broken smiles.
A tender heartbreak that is watched
by those of the unfortunate,
willing to give what's left
of their spirit to lift yours.
A child that looks up to their guardians,
feasting their eyes
on the sobbing beings.

Innocence compels them not to
understand the truth,
yet they soothe the pain with their
small hand on your knee.
Humankind is such an ugly word
that serves pure love.
All people want is to be seen by
eyes of companionship.
To be heard like a friend.
To be loved like they aren't a monster.
I believe some people
are worth sharing the pain with.
For humans have such a big heart
for nothing more but to fill it for others.

Masquerade

Copper iris's feed the electric gaze
across the flooded ballroom
to a pair of murky eyes.
Figures grazing the floor in a sweeping
motion moving like mythical
creatures from the forest.
A majestic song healing the bones of
harmonizing humans.
Their spirits intertwining
like soft vines on lumber.
The two dancers met hand in hand
as their cowl's were cloaked with a
colorful glittered mask.
The movement of their antique clothing
dashing like shooting star's
falling to the fields.
The souls caressed their way around
the room of burning smiles
fighting the flame.
In the sudden moments,
the distant piano sunk to the sound of
drowning in the roaring waters.

The arms of the mysterious bodies
cradled one another as they told stories
of their hearts by a flicker of a joyous
humane grin in their eyes.
Like they were the only warm
corpses around.
When the sound had died down
like a crackled flame,
the partners separated.
Though each of them will remember
falling in love with the touch of a
stranger at the masquerade ball.

Sheltered

Raindrops fall on the tulip petals,
while the sun arose so gentle.
And your smile burned me a fever,
all my friends said I should keep her.
The soft songs of the humming bird,
makes me feel at ease when
I lose my words.
I've learned to soften my soul,
it was always in my prophecy's scroll.
To heal with your touch of gold,
after I trembled from their
voice that was cold.
A crumbling house falling to its grave,
you sheltered me with love
I took as brave.

Not all stars burn out

He looks to her as if the stars are
invisible as they float around in a galaxy
delicately made for them.
Their backyard was quaint and soulful,
as they dream together on their rusted
metal lawn chairs
they got at a yard sale.
A red ribbon tied her hair as she
fidgets with a silver necklace he
got her for Valentine's Day.
He can't help but smile as thought
of the day he met his beloved wife.
A Polaroid photograph titled 74' rested
in the pocket of his red flannel,
always near his slow beating heart.
Letting out a mild laugh that sung of
heaven to her ears,
she looked over and saw
fate in her view.
She questions his expression,
as he slowly reaches over and whispers
in her ear past their matching gray hair.

'These are the same stars I wished
upon to get to this moment'.

Real love

The anthems of the church
bells are ringing.
Over the gloomy fogged lake
where the crows are fleeting.
A flower field stands before a storm
withdrawing from a nightmare
on the wedding day.
The choir sings with their angelic pipes
while water droplets
fill the outside ones.
Marinating shadows resting on the
benches for their time ended
before the ceremony.
A panic in the chest ruffles
the bride in a swan dress.
Barging through the wooden doors
could she taste her new life of freedom.
The residue lingering on the polished
leaves gave her a mirror that
reflected a smile.
Love doesn't have to be a human,
it just has to be real.

Something new is born

Trust me dear when I say it's love.
Eighty years from now you'll believe me
as you see my stretched marks on my
face from every time I looked at you.
I can feel my gears shifting after
all the rust started to erode me away.
Through my broken shambles you
searched my soul that still had
something good left in me.
Time twisted around us to feel
like we are immortal.
I knew from the first moment my heart
became a drum as your humor was
all the lyrics I needed.
Love truly doesn't die while I hold
your gaze that burns like fuel,
the beauty of a horizon
and the vines off a cherry tree.
It's a shame fate will send
us on different paths,
maybe one of them will lead
me back to you.

Only yours

I am fragile like porcelain waiting
at the edge of the counter.
I burn out quickly like wax melting
to a heap on the floor.
But darling,
to be deeply hypnotized by your love
that mortals confuse it with witchcraft.
To drain into a puddle because your
smile curved around my body
until it caught fire.
I follow the rules written on my palm,
though I would run away to a cottage
where we can live forever
like folk vinyl's.
I lay down my soul to match yours,
to be completely intertwined.
I would be blessed to be called your
partner as we dance around
our living room.
You deserve hand-picked flowers every
morning with love letters that will always
end in -Only yours.

Tea leaves

You're something tangy like herbal tea
on a gentle summer day.
You can tame me like a potted plant
with a vase hand made out of clay.
The burning of fire the same fiery
that glints in archer's eyes.
I'm chasing the dog around the yard
so that he knows I'll always
be around and never die.
Playing with rocks under the sunlight
since the snow melted from last Sunday.
Leave life before my brain is fried
and I start to decay.
And I'm in love with the spice of her
voice that seasons my
bane of existence.
I'm not much of a runner
but for this breeze
that holds the trees high
I would make the distance.

Something worth believing in

I worship the holy water you
were born in.
Crucified by the fixation that
is clamped to my soul.
Adored the heavenly golden blaze
tanning my fair skin absorbing
the love of the fire.
Getting drunk off your red wine hair
while I write letters from the stars
that confirm my belief of the universe.
How extraordinary to bend with the
earth and to complete someone's
other half a heart.
I'll miss my childhood home,
but time was never supposed
to stay the same.
So I will search in every crevice of life
a place that feels just as safe.
This is something worth believing in.

Stormy settlements

I'm settling in like warm rain while
the pots are burning a fever.
My head is simmering in a
light roast headache.
And I'm wondering if I will age
but never mature past seventeen.
I'm terrified of thunder,
so I'll keep my voice soft as I watch
teardrops fall down
the shuttering windows.
Resembling your quivering lip that
day we said goodbye.
But sweet lullabies are meant to
be listened while words are meant to
be kept in secret within that
old diary under my bed.
With each passing storm I hang low to
watch the grass grow to mush that helps
me know I can stand
above breaking water.
I will drain like a tea kettle puffed
with steam on a cloudy day,

leaving you to read my fortune
at the bottom of the cup.
I live as a ghost scared to move on to
the next world so I wait
until it feels complete.
Don't let me waste away and
I'll make sure you know you
aren't a waste of space.
Together we are more than any storm.

Kiss of beauty

To confront my love I bloom
inside my chest for you,
I burrow as a fox hidden
away from the world.
Even if we both contain jagged
butterflies within our bodies,
it would be best to keep it buried away
for I am but bitten frost and you are
the peeking sun over the sea.
Our eyes lock but we must never be.
If horizons ever do share our song,
for a love that was never long,
I hope the audience of the chorus finds
truth in every word.
Only if life was as simple as a sparrow
soaring above pine trees,
then I wouldn't swallow the pride that
shines when I speak of my dear.
My quill will commence with my tongue to
speak in a language forbidden
but to hold only my gaze.
Find peace where ponds never forget

to pronounce your beauty.
And I will remain captivated by the glow
of your smile and the raw touch
of happiness you fill the world with.

Lover

It's crushing the way you skate
around the block,
it's stabbing my guts of how jealous I am
over how smoothly you move.
Perhaps I'm nervous to start something
new in a time already holding
onto a cliff.
I want to be comforted by the
freedom of poetry,
ink clinging to my skin.
If I go blind as a painter with my works'
fumes dug deep in my eyes,
I will never forget how
precious you remain.
And I will never forget my parent's
arms that held my heart that raced like
a train and my eyes that
let go of rivers.
So I'm going to live how I was taught,
though my head aches of thoughts
I truly do have a heart that
just wants to love.

Burned Fables

Worm friend

The anger is suffocating.
Took a hammer and killed the drywall.
A vulnerable child awaiting
desired attention.
I snuck out to the mud puddle,
hoping to find meaning in the earth.
My shoes are flooded with soil blood,
my sweater flaked off brown dust.
Lying on the ground
came a squiggly critter.
Pink and purple it scrunched
up on my dirty palm.
I felt something real tickle my hand,
cold like the sea.
The worm scrunched around
as I was mesmerized by my child eyes.
The leaves fell slowly
when the time passed,
bitter air tasted raw in my lungs.
I sat there and I talked to you.
My new worm friend.
I told you my fears,

I told you how I hated change.
I held you as you moved
the way my mind did.
I knew we were something similar.
More connected than
I am with anyone else.
My tears dripped upon you the longer
I broke down the stone
in my throat.
Luckily,
the water held your wobbly
spine to not dry up.
We made a pack.
I help you survive,
you help me get through the day.
Because we both knew all
things come to an end.
I just wanted to stay this innocent
for a little while longer.

The birth of the phoenix

Thorns blossomed in the
throat rotting to the bone.
Drenched in tears was not enough
to wet the dry hollow spine.
Born from the flame came
an honest boy,
with a heart that weighed him down.
Every mirror vowed that he would
not be like the rest.
Careless enemies damaging the strength
of his unforgiving amount of knowledge.
Doomed to forever skip rocks in an
eternal river to reflect
his lonesome melody.
Though his hands prayed in the clay mud
to the gods that the stars would paint
him in the universe.
An open mouth that yearned to be loved
as the Greek pined of beauty
for their muse.
Came a phoenix bird that whispered
in his dreams,

they were the same.
The crave of immortal attention,
to stand out like the rainbow
over the waterfalls.
The way peace cradles
an agony of a mind.
How imagination cleverly mends
the innocence of childhood.
No manuscript could hold the boy's
fears and wants to feel included.
So they paved their own ground.
The boy and the phoenix made it their
destiny to unearth those who are
withering away beneath everyone's
unknowing heels.
A token of fate had been gifted to the
world to find where one's
heart truly belongs.

This ancient story

The sky began to clear.
The sun rose higher.
You were a sea beam,
vivid green.
Seen beyond was a plum-colored
yellow sky that dozed off.
Without a sound,
I watched the landscape.

Disease

A cream silk bedspread
with a maiden laid upon.
A feather in a river afraid to drown,
yet barely breaking the surface.
Her lungs puffed with smoke
engorging a storm cloud.
The golden crown fell to
the burnt wood floor.
Muscles dropped heavy as an anchor.
Spots of blood covering
her handkerchief,
black as mold of a sickening disease
filled her corpse.
The fading of the moon behind her
dreary eyes sinking into quicksand.
Pale as her hollow skeleton did she turn
to her frosted pane window
to see a lively songbird.
Humming a tune so soft it aches
to the Devil's ears.
A snowfall catching gently on the tree
branches that sparkled in the dawn sun.

Within the palm of her hands she held
with her remaining strength
a stargazer lily orchard.
The pleasant aroma of her mother's
perfume drifted off the enticing white
and purple petals.
A frail kiss that strained her movement
but pierced her mind with bliss.
The scene of returning home
calmed her soul.

Persephone

Oh Persephone,
daughter of mother nature
that gave us honey.
Oh Persephone,
Goddess of spring and the underworld
bringing femme fatale into the colony.
Holder of the pomegranate seeds,
painting good fortune and life for
eternity onto our palate.
To be loved by Persephone is to hold the
gaze of beauty that dies slowly
between our fingers.
Rotting ink slipping out of the forest
to rebirth a gentle swan.
Tears caress her scythe to sharpen her
hatred others feared.
Abducted by Hades,
her childhood was mistaken as a
nightmare once every full moon.
Oh Persephone,
never meant to be the evil
consumed by the good.

Oh Persephone,
in another life she was the hero.

Death petunias

Black petunias fall asleep in the
darkness of the hollow shadows.
Sweet silk gracing the velvet
wind of its body.
Jealous over the moon embracing the
other flowers dancing under
the spell of enchantment.
While cradled like a cat
who found a home.
The weakness from that kiss of poison
blinding the haze of the sun.
I too love like the flower of death.
Bringing doom to your doorstep.
Spun like a spiderweb I caught you,
secure in my arms like dried candle wax.
Gloom clouds seeping into
the late forest,
haunting the flowerbed that will never
feel peace as long as Black petunias are
resting in the soil.

Paix

Mon trésor,
je ne regrette rien.
Amour sans fin pour toujours.
Je suis éternellement jeune.
Tu es dans toutes mes pensées.
Crois en toi, intrépide et rêveuse.
Fais ce qui te semble bien.
Danse avec les étoiles.
Je suis amoureuse de mon âme sœur.
Libellule tiens bon.
Il n'est jamais trop tard.
En fin de compte tu peux le fair.

Old news

An old man burrowed in
the back of the cafe,
his ears drowned with the news.
His insides filled with black coffee
keeping him warm from the winter.
A journal rests on his table speaking like
open wounds of the current
world around him.
Sorrowness fills his golden eyes as
disbelief bites his lip.
No red flannel could hide his
disappointment with the world so he puts
all his feelings into his leather satchel
strangling his frail body.
Generations of burning the world only to
get rid of everything that could
put out the flame.

Book store memories

I fluttered around the
quaint bookstore,
clueless with innocence
cradling my tongue.
Ready to burst with the taste of
imagination in the form of ink.
Evening sun blinding the windows
into the dim rows of musty covers.
People flaking in and out letting
the bitter cold bite at my skin.
Head filled with only wind,
couldn't find the reason in
which I am here.
I peered amongst the shelves,
begging for a sign of direction
in a life of forbidden guidance.
It wasn't until I gazed upon one of
my favorite books shining its brightly
green spine to my complexion.
A pause filtered through my bones,
memories hit like a drunken midnight
car slamming into bricks.

With steady hands I captured a cold
story that melted in my fiery palms.
Turned the pages to find what I can
only explain to be profound proudness.
Annotations with hearts and stars
doodled throughout the remaining tale.
The sense of a child growing
along with the words,
somehow I saw myself through the way
this hand-me down book was
taking care of.
We all have similar stories,
kindred youth dividing our path to grow
into admirable humans.
A flicker of a smile stayed like a
portrait on my rosy cheeks.
Setting the book back to
its resting place,
hoping some kid will find meaning
between the same words.
Then I knew what my reason for that
moment was as I rejoined the open
future of the chilled world.

Countryside encounters

Grief sings on the violin.
Flushed skin burning solemn.
Take a trip on a one-way train with
creased seats and a view
of a painter's mind.
Meet a stranger that holds a story
in their cracked palms that will tell
you beauty will never be defined.
Discover a love that's like a fresh
countryside market,
bury a smile with a clementine
and white wine.
And bleed your heart on the picnic
blanket dined under the secret moon.
You'll hold her hair up and she'll steal
your jacket then whistle a tune.
Tumble down a hill where all great
inventors came to die.
Bargain with a fisherman as they are
appalled by the couple coins shy.

Become home to the innocent that want
to build with bricks a dream that could
only last in journals.
Because as you find,
the journey you seek is the only
guarantee to feel eternal.

Diary of a teenager

Try to stay hidden against the lockers
with your head pressed to the metal.
Earbuds are too deep in your ears that
they ring in your lungs.
At least at that point you don't have to
listen to your insufferable thoughts
about what others could
be saying about you.
Perhaps you are a ghost
enchanting the halls,
or maybe you're nothing at all.
With your hands dug in your pockets,
you feel like you're losing yourself.
Slowly.
Head down in the stuffy classes
while the students buzz their opinion,
you have never felt so strongly about
what they have to say.
But a chokehold catches your throat
before anything can escape
your bitten mouth.
Finding groups or crowds to feel human,

yet it seems you are only getting farther
away from finding the truth.
So by the time the bell rings,
you rush to find comfort that had been
deprived through the day.
Anything to clear the mind of an addict
that's not even high.
Days bleed into months soaking
into fresh cloth.
Somehow the fading of shadows loses
the nightmare chasing behind you.
Small steps lurking in every footprint
moving forward.
You don't have to be okay.
You just have to know that one day
everything will work out.

Tinker

Mangled parts scattered like evidence
from a crime scene about
the wooden table.
The older gentleman threw down the
crinkled newspaper in his
strained chapped hands.
The headline titled,
'Great inventor goes downhill since last
convention'.
A gruff came from his rasped voice,
he scratched wisps of silver
hair lining his head.
The closet sized cottage laid gently
lit by candles and floating dust landing
on rotting graves of old metal creations.
The soft roar of a radio resting in the
corner next to a dying cold tea pot.
For months the lights have been out
since the old man hadn't have time
to fix it.
For only invention occupied the dark
crevasses of his mind.

When suddenly a surge of bolts power
the single lightbulb swinging
above his head.
He got to work.
Hours of mutilating his fingers
and a tongue demanding
a flow of liquids,
came a little robot with a lightbulb head
and copper wires for limbs.
It's face beamed to it's birth.
The old man screamed in enjoyment
and swung his creation all around
the room with his tap-dancing.
Later at the convention,
judges laughed and mocked the little
light bulb that went dim
from all the hate.
Yet as the two went home,
they sat and listened to the radio
and made more inventions together.
Because it didn't matter if anyone
congratulated the old man's ideas.
He was proud of what he created.

Now he has someone to share his work with.

Fourth of July

The sky bursts like the splattering of
tangerine oranges of bright colors
with a sound that reminds
me of opening a can.
Makes you jump every time.
The ice cream stand stood like the flag
on the moon awaiting for customers to
mark their presence with eager smiles.
Coins rattling conversations in
the kids' pockets.
8:00 pm on the clock made time freeze
like the popsicles on our tongues,
we laid on patterned blankets that
cushioned the grass.
A concert as the fireworks became
the show,
even the crickets joined
the crowd in awe.
Trucks rolled about on *Caston* street
with their windows down and the thick
beat of rock thundering off the radio.
Cherry slushy bit my bitter tongue as

I closed my eyes and soaked
into the scenery.
Little did I know that this was the last
time I would feel like a child.

Midwestern remedies

Some days I feel I still
have more to grieve.
Peering towards the dark hues of the
shattered sky as we drive by the
reflected lake where my father
and I had gone canoeing in the
center of July as a child.
A translucent arrow nags my vital organs
from the Heavens as if saying they
understand my gilded pain.
Whispers from the radio twirl around
into my ear as I begin to recall moments
I first felt alive.
Music has always been a shadowed guide
who knew my current emotions
better than I did.
Or we pass the park that holds our
forever footprints lingering in the dried
mud from the breezy days where the
wind needed to hear our thoughts more
than our mind did.
The charming window hugs my hair

so I can make believe in a world of color
through a night that seems to repeat
like a ghost's fortune.
Perhaps I have much more to grieve,
yet I shall be proud of how far I've
come in a time that was never
easy for anybody.
There's something so poetic about living
in the Midwest sometimes.
The scenery always seems to remind you
in the moments of need.

The fiddler

The fiddler bleeds their fingers raw
while drowning in the slow pouring rain.
The skin of leather reflected off the
naked light,
the wrists of a writer that
never sees the sun.
A vacant cup that fills the lips
the same way an empty kiss does.
The fiddle cracking its strings to the
tone of fading souls.
A feeling of an absence
while scattered pennies fill the holes in
loose pockets.
They look to the sky as an apology.
Maybe tomorrow will be better,
the fiddle speaks in tongues of hardship
wanting to be more than silent music to
defy ears.

Morbid lungs

Across the bridge to
the forgotten weeds,
a cigarette lights as lungs turn sour.
An intimate glimpse of the moon peering
into the eyes of the red sea.
Remorse punishing the flesh
from a day of agony.
Veins writing sorrow into
the mouth of smoke.
It's quiet like an owl admiring the
shadows of bugs.
Bones crack to the sound of a deer
frolicking about.
Nightshade guarding the feet of a
statue buried around mushrooms.
Shivers spark conversation with the
morbid night.
Beetles and herbs cradle around the
potions consumed by the avid human
dissociated from this realm,
enjoying the hum of moth wings before
the breaking dawn.

My Lullaby

Sea shanty

The roaring of the oceans screamed
what my soul wishes it could.
Stolen secrets hidden under sea shells
that carve the sand's chest.
Dead man's treasure lies in the heart
of the hurricane shown from within.
I am the captain of my own ship,
only salty ocean tears stain
the sides of the map.
My anchor hits the coral floor,
neglected by the sea life passing by.
A siren call fading in the ominous draft.
Enough to make one go mad.
An eerie crypt of a cave sits
over so hauntingly,
an illusion of rocking in the
mysterious waves.
Who knows what creatures lie ahead.
For we all know each soul sings
of its own sea shanty.

The forgotten whisper

A pink carnation drops like a pin
to your tombstone.
I sat,
dangling my legs upon your grave,
I hope you don't find it disrespectful.
Its spring once more,
the season you have learned of rebirth.
A cardinal appears in a maple tree,
stretching its wings.
The warm breeze brushes my hair,
strands of it you have
never gotten to touch.
Blue sky is achy in my iris,
I just know you would sell your own
bones to see it.
Just you and I remain
the only souls out here.
I feel closer to you than any moment I
had met your flesh.
I'm in a garnet suit,
my ears now fit the size of my head.
You would've found that surprising.

I believe my eyes are now
glossed as diamonds,
wondering if you would've been proud
how I've grown.
I must go,
but I will look for you in every passing
moon that kisses my dreams.
I'll be quiet so you can rest now.
You may just be a faint whisper in the
back of my mind,
though I will never consider you
forgotten.

Taste of the cold

The half-moon cries the arrival
of winter.
It's getting colder.
Those words are written like
a curse on the world.
Frost eats away the green grass
that's frozen still.
Inspired by the shadows
on the pavement.
We are not alone.
Pure innocence is a delicate snowflake,
melting when the tongue of
curiosity captures it.
The season banished the light
in the afternoon.
Until it's just me underneath the
Christmas lights in the front yard
wondering when it all changed so quickly.
I'm old like the tree branches containing
memories from when I was hurt.
Flamed tears burn holes in the snow.
Maybe I'll wait here till I'm blue.

Yet this is the first time I can hear
angels sing of where I belong.

Lost kid

Envious bones weigh down my skeleton.
Digging a hole to lay all my fears in.
I drew a face in the cold foggy window.
But the precipitation drained
the drawing away,
before I could memorize its curves.
I shine like the lamppost I'm standing
under when I study your soft words,
'I'm proud of you.'
Though when you sputter
my disappointment,
I feel small like the lump in my throat
that's hard to swallow.
I cling to my sweater like I would if I
were a lost child.
Hanging onto every thread like your
attention I thrive upon.
I pulled a tarot card from
a devious deck,
finding a symbol of a withering rose.
My fortune mocked me as if I were a
jester delivering a pun.

Always to be the poet,
and never the gift of a poem.
This liminal persona traps my purity
by chasing around my tense thoughts.
For one day I shall be colored angelic
by wholesomeness,
if only I dare to be brave to conquer my
greatest enemy.
Myself.

New years

The impending tides of time have
crashed upon us.
Ready to start over the hourglass,
sinking the sand down to
the second once again.
A mentality to be afraid to withstand
a new moment,
while for others a fresh start is a
wound waiting to be healed.
Look back and evaluate over the
fondness one should feel for making
it another day.
We have learned to fail,
felt our wings break under pressure,
the smiles we wield had faded away.
Though we counted the months
on our calendars,
we found a way to get out of bed
during each season.
That's enough for now.
An achy year had came passed us,
like waves it swept us under.

But we always get back up.
Next year won't be different,
yet if you allow yourself to feel
your mind grow,
then everyday you will be granted
a new adventure.
Open your heart and perceive
your soul to fly.
Whatever the loss or love that came into
our lives in the strangest time,
we shall glow with every second ticking
to our new lives.
Don't be afraid to push
yourself this year.
It's uncomfortable at times.
But the memories are worth
more than gold.
Happy New Year.

I'm getting better

Charming moments slow dancing in my
brain while the dilation of my pupils
fixate on the moving ceiling.
The eerie sound of thunder
shuttering the house,
though I was kept stable and hidden
away like a burrowing animal.
I've found that you hate my guts,
yet I would still give up my own for you.
Crumbling from the confrontation of my
shaky voice unable to speak what my
stomach mutters.
A diary holding new names,
new meanings.
Somehow blanking on the
reason to smile.
A night around town;
a morning calling from an angel's voice.
Surrendering my cryptic beliefs to
understand that I can hold steady for
one more time.
Trapped in a wheel of the past.

Knowing I should keep my distress
to myself,
but the wish for someone to hold my
broken glass of a body.

Heaven's best friend

I can feel your velvet paws slipping
away from my palm.
I acknowledge every silver hair
pressed in your coat,
oh how your eyes still shine with life
after all these years.
No words have to be whispered when
your soul tugs on mine,
it's the loudest emotion I can hear.
We used to be the same size then I
grew up for you to be the
coziest blanket.
We experienced heartbreak together as
you watched me find who I am
in the quiet nights.
Never a day without you being
the sun waking me up.
My first best friend and forever the
last to know my childhood.
It's okay if you must go soon,
I understand.
Your breathing is resting.

You were a great dog.
Heaven will be the luckiest to ever hold
such a loyal companion.
The most strength I will ever
admire is you.
Goodbye friend,
I'll see your wings in every sunset.
I know you'll be waiting at the
Rainbow Road.

Carry on

But my thoughts drifted away
like cherry blossoms.
Through the wind I felt the erratic
scenes bury deep in my soul.
The realm of the waterfall shattered
around me breaking the sound of my
heart beating with adrenaline.
I saw magic in the chaos that was
unveiled like a treasure map when I
explored the land for the lost.
Patterns of familiar faces in the stones,
while the mountains catch my breath.
This old valley shared my stories,
compelling me with wonder that
I still have a pulse.
I found a stranger within me that I have
yet to learn of.
I love the smile people tattoo on
their young face,
though in another life I must have been
a river for how I stream my veins around
the world glorified before me.

I will carry on amidst this journey
of hidden unpredictability,
I was meant to be molded by
the hands of fate.

Buried in thoughts

I don't want to be cruel,
so I guess I'll keep my lips stitched.
I can't deny that my button eyes
have seen sin.
Oh to be the prettiest penny that
charms the wishing well.
After all I have collected,
I got no more souls to sell.
Lately you've dressed as the hunter,
and the season called me the prey.
I have lost the battle soaking
in numb bullets,
still getting war flashbacks
when we lock eyes.
Perhaps I will grow out of the lies,
the mockingbirds believe in me.
Or come to my senses to find love that
was meant for me.
For now I'll read of grim tragedies
that I learn of wise lessons.
To live is to be taught for the next life.

Born to write

The ink of the pen was born into the
palm of my hand.
Flexing the muscle of creating
literary companions.
A religious habit of engraving my
feelings with a steel blade.
As I bless the muses with comparisons
to the beauty of antique silver.
To be loved by a writer is to be
portrayed as a painting delicately gazed
by a collection of observers who need to
worship your grace.
I color my soul to match
the way sunsets fall,
so my poems can have others enjoy the
peace and pain of one's emotions.
Perhaps no one will understand my mind,
but I know I was born to write.

Time capsule

Deep in the heart of the forest,
laid dead pine needles and the aroma of
mint stinging my body.
I walked miles to enter a place
I have only marked in my dreams.
It seemed so familiar to hold the gaze
of the wilderness peering into
my aged eyes.
I dug up a molded box,
past the decaying worms
and bones of rodents.
A silver container held my past self.
I opened to smell guilt,
innocence,
and regret.
I smelled life that took a toll on me.
I sat down amongst the turning clouds to
reconnect with my younger self.
I tasted the salty tears that I could
recognize from any lonesome night that
pressed me to feel weak.

I felt a ghost of a hug push its weight on
me until I felt the way I did when I
knew I wronged you.
I saw the sunsets blind my iris on the
long summer days,
the first time I felt I had changed.
I heard my favorite songs I would
repeat on the cold shaking bus back
home when I just wanted to feel seen.
And this time I found a new scent of
mango that became a stranger
to my nose,
yet home when I smell it again.
I put the box back into the ground,
hoping I will stumble upon it once more
when I need it most.
Sometimes it's worth seeing
how far you've grown,
even if it's scary to understand.
We won't be kids for very much longer,
I had to relive my childhood
before it slips by.

The true poison

I fear evil resides within me,
so I manage to bring it out simply
because I'm afraid.
My family tree grew from a bad seed,
now we all cower that we are the same.
And I'm worried like a child with their
first loose tooth,
that you'll drift away
and I'll have no clue.
I have my father's mind with my
mother's heart destined
to compete with love.
Humanity has taught me countless
courage in a time of war.
Let's beat the odds of the darkness that
lurks in our shadow minds.
I may not die a hero,
but I will die with a brave purpose
I'm still searching for.

Bloodline

Time only aligned for a short amount of
years that we rest under the same roof.
Perhaps you watched over me for a
while and decided I needed
a friend by blood.
And our words bicker like a box
of feisty kittens,
though in an hour I look to you
as a proud sister.
Someone who would let me lean on their
shoulder during the quiet
sounds of a movie.
Someone who would share their snacks
in the back of the stacked car during a
long road trip.
Someone who can keep my secrets in a
made-up fort during the hollow night.
We may have not spent our whole
childhood together,
but fate showed me that I do in fact
want children someday because of how
honored I am to be in your life.

To my dearest brother,
you proved that this bloodline
will continue on with your legacy.

Not all ghosts are evil

I'm holding your wicker candle
while you burn low.
Supplying the matches as
the flame cries quietly.
Jumping headfirst into
the pool of melting wax,
yet you never held me back.
You sang lullabies and I believed every
sweet call of your voice.
Sugar-coded in the honey
you poured me in,
yet you never said it was enough.
Yellow jackets swarming my skin,
piercing my flesh until their venom
intoxicates my humble mind.
I used to cater poison,
provided in any mortal you desired.
Though I traded with the apothecary
for a life buried away from those who
consumed my soul.
A Bible written for me to take
a path for my own,

to let go of those who shall
haunt for eternity.
I'll sit in my grave
and wait for time to pass,
all I wish is that my tombstone
names me,
'someone who wanted to be good'.

Good guardians

The sun would drain bleak like an eternal
eclipse if this life didn't have you.
The impression of a guardian framing
the lives around you,
a saint preparing to godsend into our
homes showing us we are worth the
golden gifts of Heaven.
Taking scrap metal and turning it into
angelic trophies.
Holding a torch that lights a path of a
romanticized life,
granting keys to magical doors
of endless adventure and fortune.
A seeker of proficient kindness you
gleam off your soul.
Years of mockery in return,
though you kept climbing that tree of
opportunity and sent everyone's dark
opinions on fire.
Your stories will be painted on Ancient
Greek pottery,
the tale of a warden told in history.

I admire everything you are.
Never lose that spark in your heart,
you were meant for something amazing.

Disconnected

I feel untethered like a balloon that
was let go at the wrong time.
Dissociated from this realm during the
late-night rambles I draw on as I cannot
stand to dream of a world but to live it.
Only the touch of your ghost
interlocking with my fingers could fix my
thoughts that make
emptiness seem full.
Drowning in the energy I drank at 9
plundered down my throat and now stars
are darkening my pupils.
An embrace tangled in my blanket,
a hypnosis that failed.
I'm calling like a faint whale or a siren
that can't seem to be heard.
Give it time they say
and I will be connected again.
But how much time has passed
since they first said that?

Lionhearted

What magic had I endured to meet
someone like you.
Brave lionheart that walks as a goddess
on crystal clear water.
And you have the strength
of a dam that holds oceans,
while never giving in.
When I grow up I want to be
just like you,
challenged yet optimistic
with granted opportunities.
Perhaps our paths with continue as one
or spread like a wildfire,
but no matter where we end up,
know life will always be proud
of your smile.
May photography catch the glint of your
breathtaking admiration in the corner of
your dimples and may it
be hung in museums.
Every time I look to the window of

fog-covered mountains will I be pleased
to have ever known you.
Thank you my dear friends.
I will continue to meet those
that will encourage my love to live.

Only monsters are scared

Love has me terrified with the same
look of fear that lingers in prey's eyes.
It is unfair how I can be chaos with
so much emotion doused in my heart,
although it is a war to prepare for the
battlefield to find someone I trust.
And in the end I would find that I was
the only enemy I was facing.
I want to grow as a wilted warped tree
but I find myself alarmed to commit to
someone I hadn't known for very long.
To lay down my life and my love for
someone to possibly be there
to hear my heart stop.
Maybe in another life I'm not too scared
to love who loves me back.

Roses Carry Daggered Thorns

She hasn't changed. She only grew into
the person she's always wanted to be.
And I admire that.

I buried hearts in my iris so hopefully I
would see the world with more love.

I am at peace with my own soul. My
heart bleeds like the northern lights, I
am an open sky.

I'm still counting the constellations. Each star is a consequence I'm still understanding in my astrology books.

The soul is so kind to grow like a flower in a world of chemicals.

Seeking companionship in each familiar face is enough to grow your own library from reading everyone's stories.

There is nothing more I need in my heart, yet I can always use more knowledge for my brain and peace for my soul.

I think if you open your eyes, you'll find a bit of your soulmate in everything. That's when we learn life is our greatest love. And why it hurts so much.

Always a sorcerer that holds the poetic tongue. But never the audience who is grazed with the magic.

Eternity is the equivalent of losing the cherished night. The soul needs to rest, this is why we don't live forever.

Life isn't just one genre, so why not pursue every aspect and emotion freely to discover what it truly means to be alive.

Crimson wings will grip onto my shoulder blades, and I will never step onto the soil again.

Majestic Destinations

Dreamland

I crave the fog drifting around the ends
of the English oak trees.
The dying starlight gleams on the
resting dewdrops,
leaving a path to a repressed treehouse
withering in a quiet open field.
The land of a bleeding-heart soaking
in a chamber of eternal peace.
The way my footsteps carry a tune of
piano keys until a beautiful
symphony is created.
The marking of butterfly
kisses on my cheek,
and the gaze of innocence peering upon a
family of bunnies.
A grave of a garden with the potential
of rebirth hidden beneath the soil.
I felt the knots in my stomach loosen
and the storm inside my head is calm.
I will surrender my veins to feed the
weeds to keep my soul placed
under these comforting clouds.

I am enchanted by the everglades
that made me escape reality.

An ode to Rome

Shimmering jewels of the ocean
reflecting the ruins of the Colosseum.
Earthly art buried deep under the
forums as ghosts reenact their plays.
Marbled domes containing hidden molded
structures of the classic heroes born in
this virtuosity city.
To fall in love under the dimmed lights
on a slow boat swaying to the rhythm of
the accordion in the background.
The rich history that sinks down into
your roots until you feel
like you're home.
Standing upon the graves
of fallen warriors,
the memories of the Roman empire
inflicting our unworthy veins.
Peace was such a strange word until it
was in the air surrounding
like summer bees.
My heart was made to explore.

London love

The shelter of a modernist London
apartment shadowed upon
a quiet dimly lit street.
The scent of freshly baked bread
looming through the open
curtain windows,
while drifting off into the bellies
of rodents and stray cats.
I pause out the balcony to fill my ears
with the romantic tune of violin music
notes tapping on the cobblestone.
For a moment my heart stopped
mentioning the question
if love really does exist.
Because as my wholesome eyes felt a
moving painting being drawn out as
parents chase after
their kids on rusting red bikes.
The way their souls heal in an afternoon
than in their whole life
they experienced.

The sweet breath of laughter reviving
the dying sun setting before the clouds.
Moss setting on the stone walls where
lovers stop and admire the beauty.
And the way everyone interacts as if
they are falling in love with someone
new every second.
The way the world feels still and simple.
Longing for peace that was driven
into the characters of people.
Love is the purest definition of why
humanity remains something
to be proud of.

The mystery of the day

To be fading away like a ghostly ship
haunting the seas.
But oh to be the beaming northern lights
that serves as a compass
to the wild hearts.
Why have an ugly soul in
such a pretty life.
The stars became my friends as they
fell onto the palms of my hands wishing
me a good night then flying
away once more.
Yet I am scared to fall for the moon as
it only stares at the sun.
To captivate the spirit with endless
adventure across the atmosphere.
I yearn for the courage that you hold
within your hands.
Shall I learn bravery through every
waking moment to show I admire
your being.
To show I am proud to be taught by you.
Carry on dear souls

who loathe the world.
There's always a new day awaiting us.

It's back

The branches on the awakened trees
posture into hearts around the
strawberry sun.
The air feels gorgeous in my lungs
until I feel like I do every year when the
birds chirp more often and the moon
comes out later.
I've learned through all the seasons as
you can see the change in my eyes and
the growth in my hair.
I thought I couldn't love like I did,
but then I fell for every awkward smile
and the charm of the green grass
giggling in the wind.
This old porch holds my greatest fears
and advise me to push out my emotions
I desperately need down on paper.
The world is so beautiful when the
weather releases my numb feelings.
Just another reason why I love spring.

Artist in a past life

I want to learn how to play the guitar,
so the melodies can say what I want to
get out of my head.
Softly fumbling the strings underneath
the hollow tree,
growing leaves leaving shadows upon my
head from the evening sun.
I yearn to feel the ghosts of past
artists flowing through my veins until I
am no longer in control.
To put my dreams into a symphony and
sing it to the wind.
It's the only one that would ever listen.
Oh how I want to travel the world,
although you'll be the only
one at my concerts.
A light soul I wish could be known
as a maestro.
Or a lyrical genius that could heal the
ears of sinners.
Dear I just want to mark the world into
my sheet music,

to be seen as a musician that admires
how creative love is to be perceived.

Charlie

And the skies were no longer gray,
when the furry angel came
that very day.
Walnut eyes pressed against the leather
interior of our car,
you finally felt home upon
your chocolate fur.
We held you as we cried,
knowing you have waited
a while for our arrival.
The first to hold your paw,
and the last say how you are loved.
Without you,
our hearts beat in an empty shell.
No warmth of your hugs and kisses to
wish us good morning.
No galloping around the yard
like a free pony.
No friend to hold our tears
on a bad day.
You're not just a dog,

you're family we never
knew we needed so much.

Quaint hope

Divine nectar seeps out of the roseate
buds of newborn daisies.
A romantic melodic hum of bees circling
the realm of demure pollen,
I loathe the lucent sun being fond
of my reverie mind.
Dazed by this creative silken life,
ethereal and bewitched how my breathe
contributes to this blossomed earth.
I embrace this celestial city that prints
nobility and innocence on my fair skin.
I feel real,
nurtured from this heavenly field with
dark chartreuse leaves peering down
to my indigo eyes.
How intimate this world can be when
deviated from all the evil
that swallows us whole.
Take a moment,
watch how connected you can feel
with a touch of realism
at your fingertips.

Walking thoughts

For once I did not stare at the endless
dirt ground as I walked blindly
into the forest.
My eyes glued to the teal sky that
seemed sick by the changing weather.
And for once I did not feel
anything at all,
only this time it was different.
I felt honest to my bones.
Memories flooded in once I met the
stone arch to the opening of the park.
I did not shed a tear,
yet I felt sympathy.
No longer clueless because I'm starting
to find all the puzzle pieces
for my mind.
Connecting to souls I have not met
until I was in a tunnel of no awakening.
They showed me light,
I will show them gratitude.
Perhaps I am not the most humbling
being to ever shake hands with,

a gamble with the truth.
Trust me I've learned not to risk when
rolling the dice.
Although if I keep smiling,
I don't think I'll ever regret waking
up in the morning.
The small moments that swindle around
me until one by one we all
feel whole again.
We all matter.

Little sprout

You are your own little sprout growing
in the rich soil beneath
our humbled feet.
Planted the day you were born,
rising along your wholesome age.
Such beauty to grow up along the
foundation of nature as
the strongest wonder.
Roots as thick as dreams,
weeds of wandering thoughts turning
into proud wishes.
So many people are out for your skin,
don't let them hurt you.
Sweet sprout,
let those ponder around your garden.
Dreaming of love,
counting the stars through the leaves.
Golden dust roams your presence,
life seems to slow down
next to you small sprout.
Never give in to the fleeting storms,
stand your ground.

And when the day comes to where your
branches fall to ashes,
then leave the next sprout to
look up to you.
Some cycles of life are
worth never ending.

Elevator reflection

Clouds sheltered around
me like a new home.
Soaring straight up in a glass case
where no wind could pull me down.
I saw my crumbled reflection,
seeing bits of me that were left.
My smile was weak,
my eyes are too heavy to clearly open.
"Who was I?"
I was simply floating to nowhere
yet I pondered my existence.
"Am I real enough to continue to rise,
or shall I plunder to a puddle?"
My words seemed to be spitting
at the sun.
The most degrading thoughts are our
greatest challenger that drives the
human mind mad.
Before I could even reach
the purest of freedom,
I let my feet slip and I squirmed
out of the glass.

At the point I didn't even bother
screaming for help,
I just let my body crash
into nothingness.
Who knew we had a choice to escape
until it's too late,
everyone's last thought
is something different.

Animals are creatures too

I got a throb in my throat
like a frog with a croak.
I'm catching your tears like flies.
And I'm traveling streets hoping to be
complete by a stray cat with eyes the
size of the moon.
White daffodils and a dark horse on a
hill content with all of our lies.
A ladybug on the back of a fresh leaf.
A clownfish once spotted down
in the coral reef.
The cliche of a lion stalking its prey.
A dog afraid its owner won't make
it home one day.
So they sit and wait all alone
chewing nervously on their bones.
Crashing waves on the mother bear
and her cubs surviving off of fish.
Worried hunters will make them
their next dish.
Animals can't talk but we can hear their
grief and sadness.

We can see their expressive excitement
and times of profound proudness.
But we don't treat them as equals when
indeed they are everything
the universe calls beauty.
Take care of them.

Forever child

I don't want to miss you like
I do with temporary tattoos.
I bargain like a child in a toy store for a
love that wasn't for sale.
I want to be invincible like
the heroes on TV.
But mama said never believe
what's on the screen.
Sometimes my blanket acts like a dream
catcher for the nights I'm not strong
enough to do it on my own.
It's as if my age is messing
with my perception.
And I can never focus long enough
to pay attention.
Some days I feel the way summer leaves
breathe off their stems
to the serene atmosphere.
While on gloomy days my eyes can
mistake for something clear.
Desperate for meaning and belonging,
trying to keep my head above sea level.

To harness this confusing vessel.
I'm better off learning more
in the next life,
since I'm just a kid in this one.

Safe space

You can cry by the tulips,
enough to replenish the soil
and blossom new flowers
grown from your care.
No one ever said to be a farmer
but growth is coursing
through your veins.
Trees that admire your thoughtfulness
to strive to create more life
under the fleeting sun.
And you don't have to fix the world
as kissing the grass is enough for now.
Crochet the stars a new home in your
very hands then plant the seeds of your
dreams underneath your feet.
Slowly the earth will be everything
everyone always wished it to be.
Safe and lovely with a touch
brighter than any haven.
The world needs more people like you.

Gentle thrill

I'm covered in earthworms,
curious over your forbidden words.
I'm a garden toad shaking from the rain,
stowed away under a mushroom cap
although I can't complain.
Moss growing over my body while I sit
in the mist mistaken as nature.
Crows peck at my flesh though
I'm glad I can cater.
Oh the waterfall is majestical with
the fallen rainbow behind the pier,
the water showing my foggy complexion
from another worldly mirror.
I dangle my bones and wait for
something wholesome to arrive,
because this lonesome melody
can only deprive.
I will flourish as a rose you cut
for your darling.
I would have the prettiest coat of
feathers from a starling.
Come along and don't be shy.

This day is nothing but adventurous
as we sort through the rye.
We will float some place nice,
a world is enticed.

Wisdom Of The Young

Dangers of holding my breath

Angels cry when they see me walk with
bellicose belie.
Auspicious tendencies to captivate a
heart of a believer and the tongue
of a poet.
A true tragedy to undermine the gifts
of those that advance in empathy.
A competition with thyself to cage the
ugly deleterious beast forging
from my bones.
The innocence of a soldier defleating
from the veins I call mine.
A mastermind that loses every game.
Someday my muscles won't quiver
to my name.
But my eyes will look to the blinding
Venus and thank it for my compulsive
wishes to be grown.

A quick lesson

I'm spilling anxious words all over the
carpet from this drunken conversation.
My head being pierced like a plane to a
translucent cloud,
leaving throbbing streaks.
You're the sailboat to my ocean that
is too big to explore the ending.
I'm afraid to leave my heart
uncontrolled in a world of undeniable
needles of sorrow.
Yet learned to know whoever contains
the map to my soul shall help follow it
and are the true treasure
hunters of my endearment.

Live to be you

It felt like eternity since the ghost
has been haunting my presence.
Chained to the dungeon of this
ferocious castle.
Cemented by bricks of immaturity.
The gates were guarded
by my inner demons.
I was the only person holding me back.
I studied poetry,
I chased the clouds running
through the sky.
I sat upon the grass and watched
how the sun passes
though never changes.
I am not astrology,
I was meant more like a pure butterfly.
I must grow out of this young suit
and childlike mind to know I am able to
be something more.
If one must die for love,
would that mean we should try
to live for it too?

To let go of our caged fears.
We are never supposed to strap any
worth to our chest with an obsession.
Our skin will shine like gold once
we find how the greatest
treasure is oneself.
It's never too late to find who you are,
so don't let your regrets consume you
before you find you were always
stronger than who you used to be.
It was never your fault
life went this way.

Hatred

Saturn is slowly losing its rings.
While god's hunters are feasting off the
prey of lovers.
Inspiring cannibals that obey their cult
leader until the blood of the innocent is
written into the bible.
Earth is suffocating and participating in
self-destruction.
While the shade of a human's shell
becomes an apocalyptic showdown of
superior power.
But little do they know only one side is
truly fighting.
Spirits of the past generations paved
monumental roads that lead to a house
burning from kerosene of hatred.
To be the smallest being in the universe,
there sure are a lot of problems we
tend to scream about when it was never
in our hands to control.

You are enough

The scars in the sky spelled out the
reasons to be alive.
Perhaps there isn't a list to go by,
or a rule book to keep under your pillow.
But there are delicate strings that pull
us up when we physically
can't walk no longer,
and sanity driven by love that keeps
our reflective eyes on the scene.
People tattoo their mark on your sleeves
so they're never truly gone,
don't worry about them going away.
You'll feel them always there.
And if the dream from last night won't
stop being a broken record player,
then go for a drive where life swallows
into a real tangible feeling.
Waning in the pressure of stress,
then kiss the moon with your iris
until your soul feels raw.
It's tough to get through everyday,

yet the strength to reach your arms in
the air each morning is enough
to be proud of.
You never have to be anything more
than proud of who you
are in the moment.
There are reasons to be alive,
because you're walking the earth.
And that's enough.

Frankenstein

From a young age I had
always felt different.
The way I couldn't seem to connect to
others the way it came so easy
to everyone else.
So I broke my heart in half and stitched
it to another's to try to
make me lovable.
And as the shadows of the trees swayed
the stitches stayed,
not for long though.
Until I ended up breaking two hearts
instead of just mine.
Like a psychotic scientist I tried again,
breaking my heart into more pieces that
would combine with others.
I was a parasite consuming fragile
organs that were never meant
to be messed with.
I never did learn.
I'm not young anymore,

and all the shattered pieces wore off
until it was just mine.
My heart with broken pieces that tried
to fit to so many people and possessions
that it became a dull puzzle.
Couldn't bother to hurt anyone else the
way I abused my heart.
Aggrieved my emotions,
afraid that I was ending soon.
I'm older now,
and I've realized to only fix my own
heart instead of attaching to others.

Made for more

Let your heart sink into the typewriter,
to feel vintage love soak
on your dry bones.
Then when you're buried,
all your stories will be written
upon your body.
So you'll never be forgotten.
A needle spun your name into existence,
to make clothes others shall wear.
Then to see your beauty painted on the
walls of the Chapel.
To worship you religiously with our
tongue stuck in bleeding books.
Soft spoken the way whispers are
jealously thrown into a forbidden pond.
Burning like a star made
to grant wishes.
Always know you're meant for
dreamer's minds and artists' work.

Delicately weighted

Heavy feet traveling half a mile
and back to make it in time
to say goodbye.
Orange peel sunset with splintering rain
kissing the road.
Walking with butterflies fluttering
in my palms,
no jacket could keep them calm.
Memorized all scripts in my head
as long as it got you to stay.
Lord if there really was a God,
all I would do is pray.
To be a kid with the idea of marriage
to killing my sneakers
to tell you I'm sorry.
A storm in my lungs,
cars passed with looks of sorrow.
Let me make you proud one last time.
I'll make it worth your while.
I'm more than a fading whisper
and you are the path
I only want to roam.

Please come home.

Stuck between reality

You can curse my name to the cold,
because I never could keep you warm.
Sell your pain to my apothecary,
I'll gratefully get on my knees
and watch the blades from
your throat pierce me.
And calls from the cemetery murmur
how I can't be chained to
the fears of love,
bound to hold my feet over a cliff with
an endless bottom.
I shall not fall as long as
I try to do no harm.
A snake with moth wings,
I envy the endorsed power to heal
those with broken shields.
As I age slowly like an angel
falling to earth,
I learn I can be more than just human.
I can be anything the stars crave
in my internal veins.
That I am not haunting my shadows,

but to be reborn from the crystal light.
Eyes do deceive,
simply since we are created to prove
we are so much more
than what people say.
We are endlessly jealous of the sky
because we can't live there
until the next life.
So why not make the body
you're in proud.
Just living can do that.

Respect

The power of a voice locked away in a
tower guarded by opinions
that overrule.
An ominous adventure to retrieve
what belongs to you.
For once the cords of truth is salvaged,
lives change and moments become bigger
than all the evil.
Like a wish that is to be granted to save
humanity that has dug a hole deeper
than the sinking of the Titanic.
The journey of one's speech shouldn't
burn out their expression before even
given a chance to present
their thoughts.
It's a crime to not allow us a reason to
speak what we so delicately hold in the
palms of our hands.
Don't let anyone strangle your voice away
to a swallow,

everyone deserves to observe and
announce since we all live on the same
planet.

Coming out

Like clockwork I repeated my guilty
fears in my head as my sins.
I needed to be the good little
girl that you knew.
Because I had to convince myself
I knew who I was too.
Maybe I was always the kid
who was different.
Only wore dark clothes and dirty shoes,
secretly hoping to confuse others
of my identity.
But I tasted the metal in my blood if you
addressed my appearance and
confronted me out loud.
My knees knew shame as they met the
carpet when my forehead was practically
pressed against Heaven.
I judged my soul until I could feel
cleansed like everyone else
seemed to be.
Like clockwork it took years to
understand the colors I truly bleed.

Why has it been so hard to realize
society shown love to be anything but
free.

Stay

As an angel,
I peer with broken wings,
a world that fears they only
resonate with evil.
Venom injections flowing
through the bloodstream,
I can see it in the darkened veins caging
around their enigmatic eyes.
My angelic glow brightens the room,
though people only find the shadows
that they illuminate.
I watch as they hold up the palms
of their hands.
Each a choice their life can follow to.
Only one ends up meeting my home.
I shake my head.
This can't be true.
Though I am not capable as a fallen
whisper to make it back up,
I sit and listen.

I hear the birds entrust lyrics that
sings like an apology that life was
created this way.
I close my eyes with a flutter,
and I'm drawn to a thought.
My white dress flowing in the direction
only dreams bleed.
A question brands my mind.
'We are only meant to die,
why do we rush in times of grief?'
Our destiny is not to die but to be glad
you got a chance to live.
I open my eyes,
and I find that the one chance to find
yourself is a hard concept
to understand.
We are afraid that we hold evil
within ourselves,
we decide to give into it.
It's not your fault minds
are so troubling.
Hearts should never have to cry as hard
as a broken angel.
It will get better,

even if it's not that easy.
A spirit is always watching,
hoping you make it.
Live to show them you can
continue on their glory.

Fever dream

You're something familiar like a swing
swaying off an enchanted tree.
Blue fog catching fireflies with the
smell of burning wood
passionately igniting.
I might be luck with the hazy teal
crystal wrapped around my neck.
March captivates the lucid dreaming
that's tucked up my sleeves.
I'm worried to get a paper cut so I hold
your fragile skin gently.
The river's musk is crying while the
bronze blaze of the torch you carry
whimpers to a fade.
Bury the lust and thorns attached to
your jaw and I will keep watch from the
nightmares stalking our footprints.
Mistake death as if we aren't prisoners
born from the wild.

Life enjoyers

Make the mistakes that become a
permanent tattoo on your story.
Dance blindly underneath the stoplights
that gleam in the rain.
Become a visionary of your own art that
can be hung wherever it is desired.
Because the clock ticks down faster for
those who don't care to
enjoy the moment.
But seconds stand frozen as smiles stay
like a portrait glued to your memories
if only you dared to feel complete in
that instant.
Lose the air in your lungs
when you see something stunning.
Break your hands completing something
you're proud of.
And never forget to just be something
you will always admire.
It's never too late to shine
like summer waters.
So live like no one is watching.

Interlude

It's terrifying when thoughts inject
like shots of feeling trapped.
I have a list of To-Do's dangling
from my pocket,
yet I just want to commence my feet to
run along the fields that seem nostalgic
with my headphones deep in my ears.
To hang under the mistletoe and kiss the
poison that drips down
to my chapped lips.
One day I'll be buried,
for now I walk along the spot that will
one day hold me.
I want to fall in love the way it feels to
spin around and almost hurl
from being dizzy.
Sweet dreams may be so healing and
therapeutic but to live is to feel real and
catch the soft whispers
of what it means to be alive.
I have so much more to accomplish
and so many moments to experience.

So here I am,
just a writer who yearns to learn to
never let go of the present.

Surprise Short Stories

To be seen is to be admired

The sun is setting behind the dying number of green leaves on the naked trees throughout the forest. Animals are scattering around, and what is left of the birds in this chilly fall evening, are chirping about. A lonesome pale boy in dark clothing sits awkwardly and kept away from the world on a lone bench. He has headphones on and is deeply intrigued in his notebook. His face is solemn and tired, he keeps scratching

the same phrase in his beat-up notebook

nervously. 'I am enough'. When a sound

catches his attention as he looks to see

a group of smiling teens beyond him

having fun.

They don't seem to notice him, but

he grows more pain beyond his eyes.

Without looking back at his notebook, he

closes it and gets up. Keeping his head

down, he heads towards the woods.

Ignoring the laughter he's walking away

from. He is alone, hands in his pockets,

past the bare trees. The scene looks

golden as the sun flares and spreads

throughout the forest. Such a

wholesome sight, but the boy still lingers

his head to the ground of crushed

leaves. The silence makes the boy feel at

ease. He feels like he made it home. If

he ever knew what home was. He finds a

sturdy dark trunk of a tree and leans up

against it. His dark hair fell perfectly

against it. The boy thinks he is feeling the earth spin alone.

The crackle of a leaf makes him jump. A beautiful girl enters as if angels are singing. The angelic glow of the evening sun reflects off her light hair. Her face looks wise. Wide lips into a smirk of hidden secrets. Her eyes sparkle like a pond waiting for someone to explore. The flick of her eyebrow made what she was thinking like a distant memory. The boy was astonished, a knot captured his throat. His eyes grew out of wonder. His pulse quickened with his hands beginning to fidget. "Do you also enjoy the warmth of silence during a cold evening?"

The girl spoke as you would expect a piano to strike a conversation. Her arm leaning against the tree trunk as the boy melted under. The boy blinked to his amazement. His mouth was a wide moon. "I know silence. And I wouldn't suggest it as warm."

The boy mumbled. His head facing the ground once more. The girl could tell his concern that consisted of a tangled mind. The girl made another smirk that seemed to state that she understood his pain. She nodded carefully. She put her hand underneath his chin, pulling it up to the sky.

"Well, the problem is that you're always looking down. The world is meant to be admired."

Her voice was soft like honey, trailing on with the wind. The boy's dark eyes felt full. Life seemed to bloom in his iris. The first time he had ever felt that.

"Before it gets dark, I need to show you something, while we still can see it."

The girl moved her smooth hand to meet the boy's sweaty palm. Without a word he followed. It felt like he could already trust her. The sun fell into the quicksand of a dark abyss. Hand in hand they ran up a big hill in the forest.

Laughing as though they were drunk. The

grass cleared a path as it swayed by.

They made it to the top of the hill where

peace was a grave in how silent it was. A

comfortable silence. The hill was just of

crushed leaves and frosted grass blades.

Their silhouettes danced like shadow

puppets. The two tackled each other like

playful kittens onto the ground. They

fell as their lungs burned of fire from all

the running, as their ribs broke in from the laughter.

The sky was now black felt with snow droppings splattered about. The stars had risen poetically. The two teenagers laid flat on the cold ground, their heads throbbing uncomfortably but their hearts told them to stay. The girl looked over at the boy with a hint of sparkle that shined, brighter than the stars combined. The boy looked back, trying to hide the fact his soul was screaming excitedly. He's never gotten this close to someone, let alone a pretty girl. He was the first to speak what the universe put in his mind.

"Do you just let any stranger follow you into the dark?"

He laughed awkwardly in an innocent manner.

"Funny. It feels like I've known you a lifetime."

She looks back to the sky with a subtle smile. This felt like a dream.

"Oliver. My name is Oliver."

The girl looked back to the boy

that now has a name to his charming

face, though behind his eyes he still

seemed pained.

"You seem unsure." She answered back.

"Sometimes I forget I am even worth a

name."

He chimed back in a sad call.

Making his eyes wander back to the dim

moon. He thought to himself how this is

it. She could never love him because of how weird he appears to be.

"Violet. My name is Violet."

He looks back at her astonished, the same way when they first met.

"And the stars help me remember I have a name."

She says again in a fleeting smile. Like she told a big secret she hasn't told anyone else.

"What makes you feel alive, Oliver?" Violet questioned.

Now leaning on her elbow and side so she can face him. Oliver thought for a second. Questioning everything he has ever experienced. This was the one burning question that made him ponder who he really was. Oliver thought about his key moments when he felt alive. He thought about writing in his journal for hours upon hours alone in his room under a fading lamp. He thought about walking on the train tracks, one step in front of the other trying to balance under the fleeting sun. He thought about the time

he ran away from his home during the

midnight of a cold Saturday. Only the

lamppost guiding his way home. He could

hear his father calling from blocks away

to stop, but nothing could've stopped

him. Not even his tears. He thought

about the school dances where he sat

alone under the disco light away from

everyone dancing. The music circled in

and out of his mind. Oliver thought about

how he got into a fight one time when

kids in his grade found him after school

and punched him until his nose bled and

his eyes only saw fuzzy hazes.

"Existence. Because all the pain makes

living seem poetic and worth trying at

least once."

Oliver managed to whisper through

cold tears forming from the flashbacks.

His face revealed he finally realized

that he was just a kid trying to find his

way.

Olver had gone home and laid across his messy bed. He grabbed his journal that had the same chicken scratch message 'I'm not enough' to write the first different message with a hand that was finally stable.

'My name is Oliver, and I am enough.'

He closed the journal and placed it on his wooden nightstand carefully next to his action figures. He looked out his window to the darken night. The first time he took a deep breath with fresh air in his lungs. His face was sallow from the illuminating lamp on his skin. His wholesome eyes peered at the moon. Standing in his fully lit room. "Thank you, Violet. I now know my name."

He whispered with a small smile that told a thousand words. Oliver then climbed into bed and turned out the lamp. It was the first time he had good dreams that night.

We are born to be forgotten?

"I write because it can make others feel what I cannot."

The husky voice seeping from thin cracked lips pronounced in a low tone reading from a cornered-torn paper. Black pin-striped suit covering the man's broad shoulders that sagged like the winter trees outside the glowing window that seemed to illuminate the depressing room.

Dark eyes fell like a dim waterfall across from the narrow man. She wasn't crying, she was drawing her watery eyes to hold up a dam from all the emotions she was hiding in her head. The silence grew of fog that was made for a horror movie, she felt she was living in one. The man set down the pale form he had firmly been holding onto the stable oak table filled with neatly made with pens and files. A hidden secret laid beyond his grimace, and she did not have a key to unlock his troubled thoughts.

"Here at this institute of a fine University, one must be more than a writer that 'makes others feel'. One must portray their own holy grail of passion."

There was no emotion to the man's wrinkly tight features. Even his dark brown hair remained in perfect slick back form every time he swayed. Her back slouched on the stair, unamused.

The girl even focused on the way his

moles bounced when he furrowed his

brows, almost slipping up with a smile of

her distraction.

"With your background, I know you can

be so much more. Until then, you will not

be enrolled into this school."

The man stood tall that made a

church seem small. He fixed his tie and

coughed, watching with his soil eyes of

soaking dirt as the girl saw nothing but

imagination past her pupils. Her legs

dangling in the fragile wooden chair, her

nose pointing at the hand-painted

portraits around the dark amethyst walls

that comforted the morbid mind.

"We will meet again, Ophelia."

He presented his arm out towards

the door of which she regretted ever

coming in. Ginger bangs flew around her

oval head as she turned with stitched

lips. A light green flannel wrapped

around her waist flowed with anxiety.

She had learned from the man to not show emotion just as he did. Because why present anything other than anger?

The hallway at the main campus was a drawn-out sun-filled hell. The way the sun poured in without asking through the light-yellow stained windows. Ophelia's converse were the only shoes to speak down the wooden floors. She made it out to the cold that hit her sleeveless black shirt endlessly with hammers.

I know who I am. There is nothing

more to find.

Her head felt sunken underneath

the dark reservoir that is located right

next to her house. It feels almost as if

angels speak to her at the peak of dawn

when her body is just starting to wake

up to the smell of black coffee and the

hum of the wind singing to the rising sun.

Any normal day she would have gone

right home to take back the sleep she

had missed for that insufferable

meeting with the Headmaster of *Coalix Academy.*

It wasn't even worth it because she didn't get in with her love for writing. She is not enough. That's the only reason she can come up with. Yet today Ophelia feels the tendency to go on a walk to everywhere and nowhere all at once. To escape to a world of her own and no one else. Since she moved to a different country, it has been just her anyhow. Why start letting others in now? She thought this would be the perfect

chance to work on her writing, she was

sure would never take off.

The ground held her feet gently

once she stepped off the cooled

pavement to the squishy home of leaf

graves. She left the dark academy and

didn't want to look back. Her mother

always said,

'You cannot look back on failure, but

instead find a path that will help you

understand why you ever felt you would fail.'

Perhaps her mother was the wisest person she had ever known. The bare trees remind her of her mother the way the branches may appear frail yet have the strength to carry on through every season. Ophelia continued past the light falling snow that kissed her freckles, she made sure she was just as brave as the bravery she was shown her whole life. Whispers of hollow dreams begging to be fulfilled wandered the bitter air,

she counted the number of times she

felt inspired. But quickly her ideas

expired like every great artist on their

deathbed. Her nose twitched to the cold

and her eyes had a modernized magic

spark pursuing her iris. Ophelia

wandered past the rickety old wood

bridge dusted with powdered snow that

reminded her of fallen battles from the

history books she studied meticulously.

Frozen waters below waiting for spring

to unthaw its angelic glow. The way the

sun reflects off the frozen tundra of

crystals made the scene look as if it was

captured for a movie. Or Ophelia was

lost in one of her favorite fantasy

books.

Her shoes took lightly across the

bridge as she never thought to look

down, but to keep her head straight and

ready. She had made it to another path

of rows occupying pine trees coddling

the path with pine needles and

frostbitten flakes. And like the faith in the fire to a poor man's belly, her soul caught delight. Something familiar in the light white glow blending with emerald. It was like one of her father's paintings coming alive. The mind of a painter stood creativity jealous of the way a human heart can capture such emotions in a moment that never passes.

Ophelia was always proud of her father for the dedication he had maintained through the years of hardship only a true sailor endures. Her

eyes closed for a passing second to

almost hear his voice in the way he was

so passionate in his work. She wanted to

be like him, the aspect of a gifted mind.

She walked on alone as if the spirits

compelled her to keep reaching her

destiny if she only moved forward.

Ophelia waited for ideas to strike her

like a lightning bolt letter addressed

from Zeus. Yet nothing felt right. She

wondered how things could be so easy

for those when they succeed, and if she was the lonesome of the world whose dreams were never meant to be reached.

The temperature dropped although her arms felt breathable without being covered. Almost as if the cold made her feel sober at a time that made her mind drunk. Songs from her favorite bands replayed in her head which made her feel like a friend was serenading her. Around the corner, there was something brand new just as before. Like no matter where you can explore there is always something waiting to be seen and perceived from a new perspective.

Something began to startle the covered bush nearby. Ophelia seemed engaged, but jumped a couple inches back, her breath leaping into a warm fog out of her lungs. Within a couple of silent moments a small *meow* drove her heart into a longing sensation. Her lips drew an upward arrow on each side when her pupils danced like the bright moon

reflecting in the water. The fur of a

velvet night purred with tiny flakes

falling to its tight skin. The cat looked

like a full night sky. Ophelia dropped to

her knees as the cat's clover green eyes

hesitated to get closer. She held out

two fingers close to the cat's whiskers.

Its nose twitched as it finally gave in

and rubbed its face against her palm.

They both felt at ease.

Ophelia finally registered that this furry companion reminded her of her brother back at home. Sleek and charming with a heart of pure innocence. She always wished she had the patience and hesitation to emotions as he had always had. The two creatures sat together as if they were two fish wanting to catch the stars on the surface of the water together. Together it was just them. She felt even more at home.

Suddenly her mind was filled with ideas that could fill journals which she stored under her twin-sized bed. Her lungs pumped rapidly as her cheeks blushed with excitement. Perhaps she had learned something about herself from this walk after all. And perhaps she could achieve her dreams as a writer if only she reflected upon what truly makes her dedicated to write. Ophelia petted the cat and dashed back towards the academy. The cat watched her every move as her legs flexed onto a path of

fire with the clashing snow.

For her walk took a good amount of

time to get through, she made it back to

the school in a matter of minutes. Not a

shortened breath that broke out of her

mouth, but passion striking through her

body. Adrenaline was her moment to

catch the future before it was too late.

Ophelia walked the same path of the

tiring depressing hallway to the

headmaster's wooden doors that bulged

out towards the sun like a sunflower.

She pushed open the doors eagerly, her

hair sticking to her flushed forehead.

The man with broad shoulders that

she had seen many times before, was

even more startled than when she first

met the cat. He stared with his sunken

eyes that could've been feet down into

his grave. She gave a smirk before

applying what she was going to say. The

first words she had actually said out

loud in a long time for only thoughts took all her strength to feel.

"Oh, but I am passionate. I thrive off a vine that dwells towards the sleeping sun. I can make it far in this world, I can and will be so much more than a writer that can 'make others feel'. Because from what I learned from my past and the connections I have made and what makes me up, I know I want to write so I will never be forgotten. That is why we pass down stories anyway, right?"

She paused almost regretfully to stand up to a man she had never seen emotion be born in. The man looked down to his polished shoes with a slight chuckle. He looked back up to see the timber of fire burning from Ophelia's eyes.

"You will do great. Not only in this institution, but in this life. You will inspire many as a writer, may you never be forgotten."

Dear friends,

For a moment I did not know what I wanted to be when I grew up. Truthfully, the future seems so far away, yet we reach that time with each passing second. I pondered my existence, which can be a lot to handle at such a young age. It was not until I discovered how my writing can heal what's ugly in my mind. I found how I deeply fell in love with the experience to write, create, and imagine in a world of my own that I get to share. As a human, I struggle with feeling normal and the right amount of emotions. And honestly, I can not tell if it will ever get better. But I know I can continue to share my thoughts to those who possibly also feel lost. Everyone deserves to connect to something. I thought I was going to write a different book at this time, yet I had more words I needed to get out. Lately life has seemed so precious and fragile that I'm worried it will break as soon as it falls. No one should have to live in fear. I have been confused about who I am for a very long time. Slowly drowning in the dark, but I'm getting better. Honestly, I find the little things in life to be my most favorite. The one song that can not get out of your head. That first sip of my favorite coffee while the windows are down. That sunset that steals my soul with its gaze. I think we always have a chance to grow up, though sometimes it's nice just to be where we are in the moment. Just to breathe and ponder how incredible it is to even have a heartbeat. I contribute this book to many people that are close in my life, I hope you can relate. I dedicate this book to my family who never gave up on me despite how often I changed my dreams or cried because I'm still not sure of the path I'm heading in. I want to thank my friends, the old and new. While the world seems to drift on without me, you made sure I was pulled back into reality. Made sure I was never forgotten. I have so much more I would like to write. So many more stories I can't wait to infuse into the world. I am just starting to make my mark out there. I'll meet you again my friends in the next book. All I have left to say is I am Novalee Burkett and I am someone I admire.

-Novalee Burkett

The world is something special
with you in it.

Check out other books by
Novalee Burkett...

The Monster Guild
Frightful Features
Oakheart Adventures
Growing up to be.

Follow on Instagram
@thewriternovaleeburkett

More books coming soon!